HOW TO DRAW
MAGICAL
CREATURES
AND MYTHICAL BEASTS

Mark Bergin

PowerKiDS
press

New York

Published in 2009 by The Rosen Publishing Group, Inc.
29 East 21st Street, New York, NY 10010

Editor: Rob Walker
U.S. Editor: Kara Murray

Library of Congress Cataloging-in-Publication Data

Bergin, Mark.
  Magical creatures and mythical beasts / Mark Bergin. — 1st ed.
      p. cm. — (How to draw)
  Includes index.
  ISBN 978-1-4358-2518-5 (library binding)
ISBN 978-1-4358-2647-2 (pbk)
ISBN 978-1-4358-2659-5 (6-pack)
  1. Art and mythology—Juvenile literature. 2. Animals,
Mythical, in art—Juvenile literature. 3. Drawing—Technique—
Juvenile literature. I. Title.
  NC825.M9B47 2009
  743'.87—dc22

                              2008002332

Manufactured in China

Contents

4   Making a Start

6   Perspective

8   Using Photographs

10   Materials

12   Sketching

14   Centaur

16   Dragon

18   Gryphon

20   Hydra

22   Minotaur

24   Pegasus

26   Phoenix

28   Troll

30   Unicorn

32   Glossary, Index, and Web Sites

Making a Start

Learning to draw is about looking and seeing.
Keep practicing and get to know your subject.
Use a sketchbook to make quick sketches.
Start by doodling, and experiment with shapes and
patterns. There are many ways to draw; this book shows
one method. Visit art galleries, look at artists'
drawings, see how friends draw, and — most
importantly — find your own way.

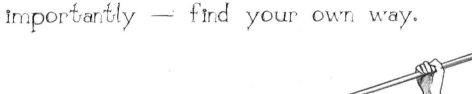

Centaur

Remember that practice makes perfect.
If a drawing looks wrong, start again.
Keep working at it — the more you
draw, the more you will learn.

Dragon

Minotaur

Pegasus

5

Perspective

If you look at any object from different viewpoints, you will see that the part that is closest to you looks larger, and the part farthest away from you looks smaller. Drawing in perspective is a way of creating a feeling of space — of showing three dimensions on a flat surface.

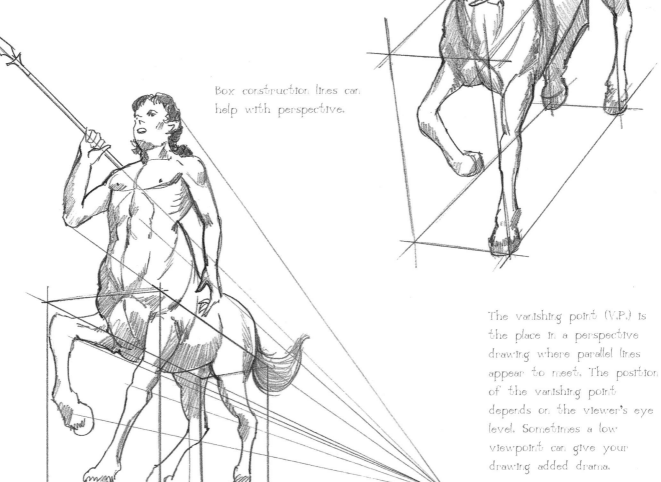

Box construction lines can help with perspective.

The vanishing point (V.P.) is the place in a perspective drawing where parallel lines appear to meet. The position of the vanishing point depends on the viewer's eye level. Sometimes a low viewpoint can give your drawing added drama.

V.P.

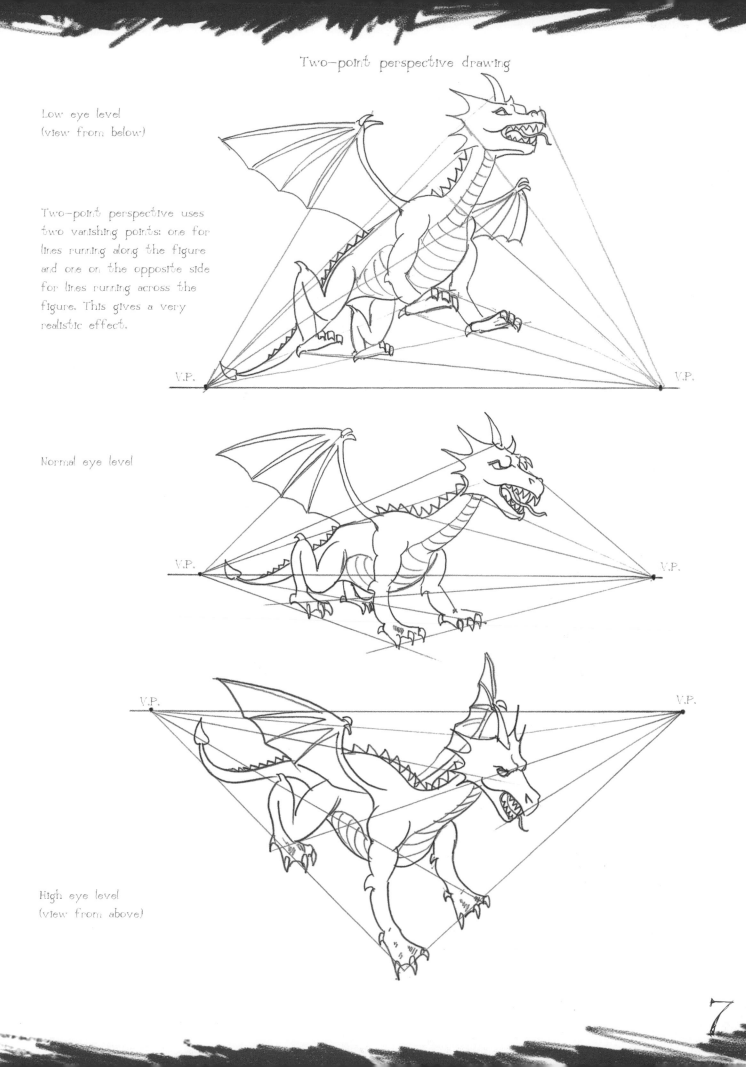

Low eye level
(view from below)

Two-point perspective uses two vanishing points: one for lines running along the figure and one on the opposite side for lines running across the figure. This gives a very realistic effect.

V.P.

V.P.

Normal eye level

V.P.

V.P.

V.P.

V.P.

High eye level
(view from above)

7

Using Photographs

Drawing from photographs of real people amd animals can help you identify shape and form. This will help make your imaginary creatures more realistic.

Drawing from photographs

Make a tracing of a photograph and draw a grid of squares over it.

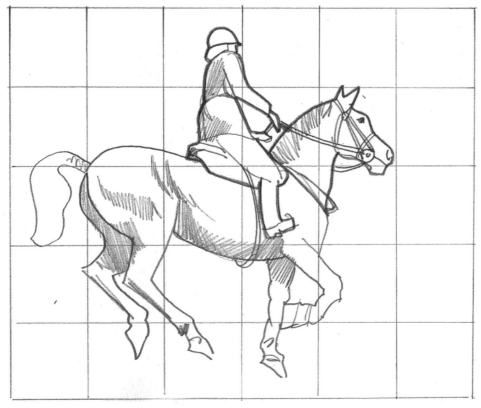

Now draw another grid on your drawing paper, enlarging or reducing the squares but keeping the same proportions. You can now transfer the shapes from each square of your tracing to your drawing paper, using the grid as a guide. Draw only the parts you want to copy — in this case we don't need the horse's head or the rider.

Now you can draw in the centaur's upper torso in any pose you want. Use simple ovals and circles to sketch in the head and arms.

To make your drawing look three-dimensional, decide which side the light is coming from so you can put in areas of shadow.

Sketch in an overall tone and add ground texture to create interest and a sense of movement. Pay attention to the position of your drawing on the paper. This is called composition.

Materials

Try using different types of drawing papers and materials. Experiment with charcoal, wax crayons, and pastels. All kinds of pens, from felt—tips to ballpoints, will make interesting marks. Try drawing with pen and ink on wet paper.

Ink silhouette

Try cross—hatching. This is when pencil lines crisscross one another to slowly build up and develop tone.

Remember, the best equipment and materials will not necessarily make the best drawing, practice will!

Hard pencils are grayer and soft pencils are blacker. Pencils are graded from #1 (the softest) to #4 (the hardest).

Felt—tips come in a range of line widths. The wider pens are good for drawing in large areas of flat tone.

Drawing pens can be used to do a cross—hatching technique for tone.

Charcoal is very soft and can be used for big, bold drawings. Spray charcoal drawings with fixative to prevent smudging. Fixatives should be used under adult supervision.

Pastels are even softer than charcoal, and come in a wide range of colors. Spray pastel drawings with fixative to prevent smudging.

Wax crayons can be scraped away from parts of a drawing to create special effects.

Lines drawn in ink cannot be erased, so keep ink drawings sketchy and less rigid. Don't worry about mistakes, as these will be lost in the drawing as it develops.

11

Sketching

Y ou can't always rely on your memory, so look around and find real—life things you want to draw. Using a sketchbook is one of the best ways to build up your drawing skills. Learn to observe objects: see how they move, how they are made, and how they work. What you draw should be what you have seen. Since the Renaissance, artists have used sketchbooks to record their ideas and drawings.

Try drawing models of people and animals. It is good practice for your observation and understanding.

There are many places
to observe animals,
from pets at home to
animals in fields.

Drawing pets is a
good way to study
their movements,
muscles, and anatomy.

A quick sketch can
often be as
informative as a
careful drawing that
has taken many hours.

Centaur

A centaur is half horse and half man. Centaurs were said to have come from the mountains of Thessaly, in Greece, and were wild, lawless, and savage. The Greek hero Heracles killed centaurs with poison-tipped arrows.

Draw in a rectangle for the centaur's chest.

Man body

Draw two circles to form the body.

Draw in the center line

Draw in lines for the back and the belly.

Horse body

Draw the ground the centaur stands on.

Draw a line for the spear.

Head

Spear

Draw a small circle for a head and two lines to form a neck.

Arm

Front legs

Back legs

Add lines for the legs and arms, with circles for the joints, hands, and hooves.

14

Indicate the positions of the eyes, nose, and mouth.

Draw in the muscles of the upper body.

Add detail to the centaur's hands.

Add hair to the centaur's head.

Draw in the muscles of the lower body and curved lines to show the position of the tail.

Draw in the detail of the spear.

Finish drawing in the eyes, nose, and mouth.

Shade in the muscles.

Pencil lines should follow the direction of the tail.

Take a look at real horses' legs.

Composition

Use squares or rectangles to frame your composition. This can make all the difference.

Dragon

Dragons are thought to have magical and spiritual powers. They are common to many cultures of the world. These cunning creatures typically have scaly bodies, wings, and fiery breath. The Chinese consider them symbols of good luck.

Draw a circle to form the head and a larger oval for the main body.

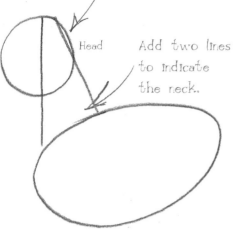

Head

Add two lines to indicate the neck.

Main body

Sketch in shapes for the top of the head and the lower jaw.

Draw in lines for the wing base and circles for the joints.

Add a long, curved line to show the position of the tail.

Head

Draw triangular shapes to indicate the positions of the feet.

Add lines for front and rear legs, with circles for the joints.

Chiaroscuro

The use of light and dark to create bold images is called chiaroscuro. Try this on the dragon to get more impact.

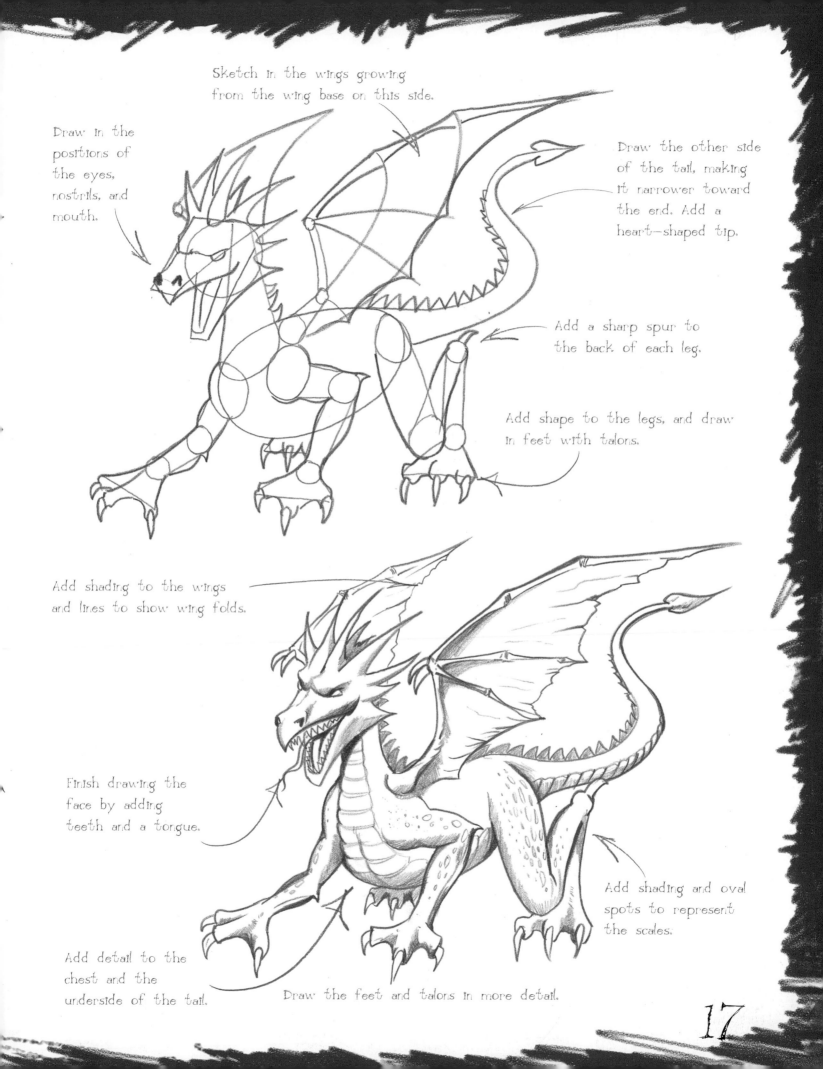

Sketch in the wings growing from the wing base on this side.

Draw in the positions of the eyes, nostrils, and mouth.

Draw the other side of the tail, making it narrower toward the end. Add a heart-shaped tip.

Add a sharp spur to the back of each leg.

Add shape to the legs, and draw in feet with talons.

Add shading to the wings and lines to show wing folds.

Finish drawing the face by adding teeth and a tongue.

Add shading and oval spots to represent the scales.

Add detail to the chest and the underside of the tail.

Draw the feet and talons in more detail.

17

Gryphon

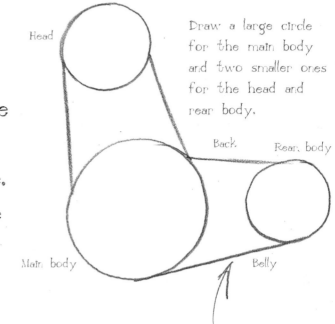

The gryphon, or lion—eagle, was considered to be the king of the air and was a powerful and majestic creature. In Persian culture, gryphons are shown pulling the sun across the sky.

Head

Main body

Back

Rear body

Belly

Draw a large circle for the main body and two smaller ones for the head and rear body.

Draw in lines for the neck and for the back and belly.

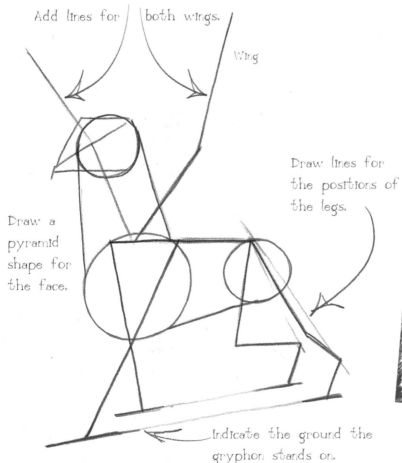

Add lines for both wings.

Wing

Draw a pyramid shape for the face.

Draw lines for the positions of the legs.

Indicate the ground the gryphon stands on.

Negative Space

Look at the space around the figure (negative space) to help check the proportions and shape of your drawing.

Wing construction

First draw two straight lines.

Add two oval shapes.

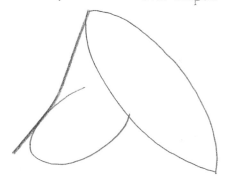

Add muscles to the wing.

Indicate the groups of feathers.

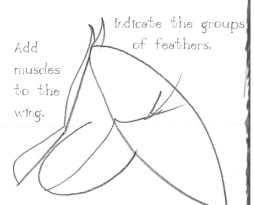

Carefully draw in rows of feathers.

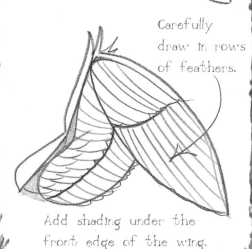

Add shading under the front edge of the wing.

Carefully sketch in the beak, then add ears and eyes.

Draw in a shieldlike shape at the base of the body.

Add detail of back feet and legs.

Add a curved, lion-like tail.

Tail

Sketch in the front feet.

Add wing features (see left).

Finish drawing the detail of the gryphon's head.

Use short downward strokes to draw the chest feathers.

Add shading.

Add hair to the tip of the tail.

Draw the sharp eagle's talons.

Hydra

The Hydra in Greek mythology was said to guard the entrance to the underworld beneath the waters of Lake Lerna. Heracles killed this hideous creature as one of his twelve labors.

Add two lines to join this leg to the body.

Draw a large oval for the main body.

Main body

Legs

Draw four tube shapes for the legs.

Draw a circle for each of the Hydra's nine heads.

Head

Neck

Main body

Draw long, curvy neck lines from the back of each head to the body.

Lightly sketch in a long, wavy line for the tail.

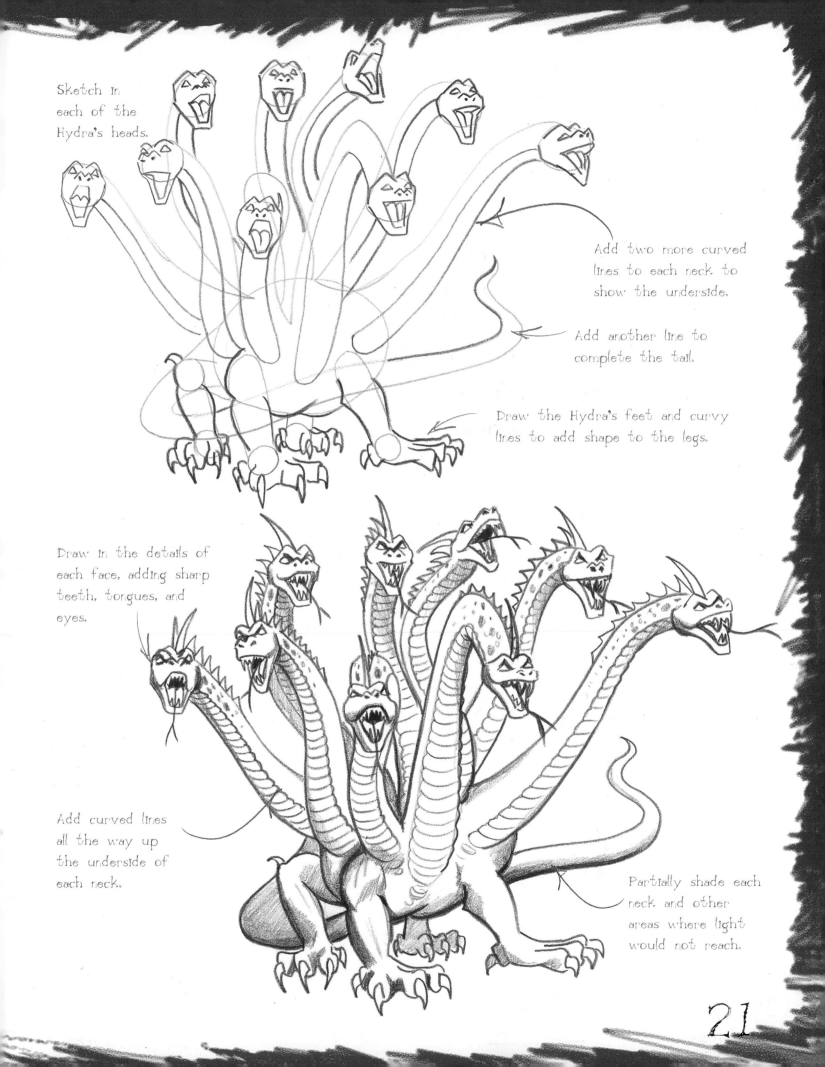

Sketch in each of the Hydra's heads.

Add two more curved lines to each neck to show the underside.

Add another line to complete the tail.

Draw the Hydra's feet and curvy lines to add shape to the legs.

Draw in the details of each face, adding sharp teeth, tongues, and eyes.

Add curved lines all the way up the underside of each neck.

Partially shade each neck and other areas where light would not reach.

21

Minotaur

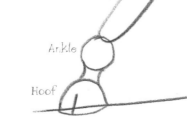

The Minotaur was half man and half bull. This creature from Greek mythology was said to dwell in the labyrinth constructed by King Minos at Knossos. Theseus eventually killed the beast, then found his way out safely by following the trail of string he had left to guide him.

Draw a vertical line through the center.

Head

Sketch in two circles and an oval to form the head, main body, and hips.

Main body

Hips

Center line

Center line

Head

Arms

Draw a line to indicate the tops of the shoulders.

Draw a straight line passing through the hand shapes for the axe haft.

Sketch two ovals, one smaller and overlapping the other, to show the right arm bent at the elbow. Add a circle for the hand.

Hips

Sketch a long oval shape with a roundish oval below it to show the foreshortening of the left arm. Add a smaller overlapping circle for the hand.

Thigh

Lower leg

Ankle

Hoof

Draw a large oval for each thigh. Add two lines to join these to the smaller ovals that form the lower legs. Add circles at the end of each leg for ankles, and sketch in the hooves with two semicircles.

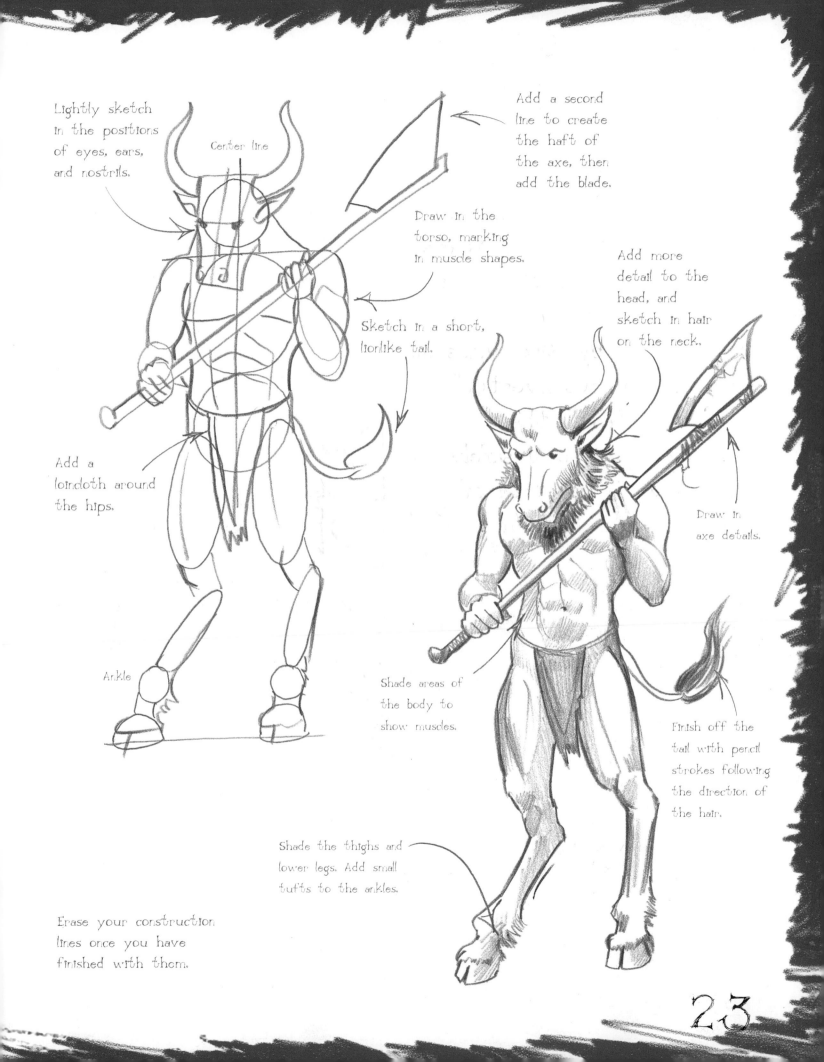

Lightly sketch in the positions of eyes, ears, and nostrils.

Center line

Add a second line to create the haft of the axe, then add the blade.

Draw in the torso, marking in muscle shapes.

Add more detail to the head, and sketch in hair on the neck.

Sketch in a short, lionlike tail.

Add a loincloth around the hips.

Draw in axe details.

Ankle

Shade areas of the body to show muscles.

Finish off the tail with pencil strokes following the direction of the hair.

Shade the thighs and lower legs. Add small tufts to the ankles.

Erase your construction lines once you have finished with them.

23

Pegasus

Pegasus, the Greek winged horse, was said to have been born from the blood spilt by Medusa's murder. Pegasus aided the Greek hero Bellerophon against the Chimera and the Amazons. He also brought thunderbolts to Zeus, the king of the gods.

Draw a triangular shape for the neck and a circle for the head.

Head

Back

Rear

Belly

Draw two circles, one slightly larger than the other, for the body. Add lines for the back and belly.

Draw three lines from the head and another line across to form the muzzle.

Draw a crooked line to indicate the front wing base.

Sketch in a V-shaped line to show the base of the neck.

Draw lines for the directions of the front and back legs.

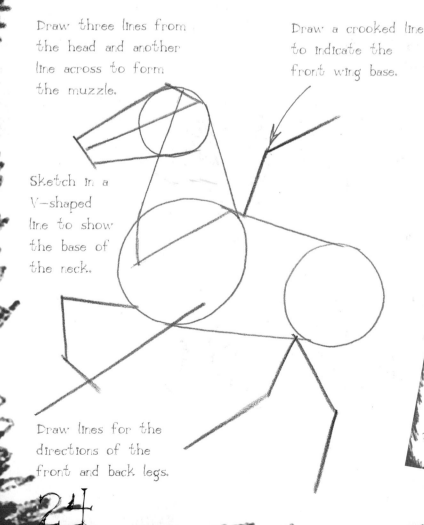

Proportion

To keep the object you are drawing in proportion, choose a unit of measurement that you can relate back to. Here the width of Pegasus has been divided into three. You can also mark key points in the drawing to take measurements from.

Wings

Draw a bent line for the front of the wing.

Draw a simple curved shape for the main part.

Add the inner part of the wing.

Indicate the rows of feathers.

Neatly draw in the overlapping feathers.

Sketch in the horse's eyes, mouth, nostrils, and ears. Add a mane.

Draw in wing shapes.

Indicate the flowing tail.

Draw in more lines to give the legs shape. Add circles for joints.

Add more detail to the horse's head.

Draw small wing feathers first, then draw longer feathers.

Shade in the muscle shape.

Add more detail to the tail.

Shade in the underside of Pegasus to create a three-dimensional effect.

Phoenix

The phoenix is a mythical bird said to live for up to 1,461 years. It has red and gold plumage. Each time it nears the end of its life, the phoenix builds a nest of cinnamon twigs that ignites. Both the bird and its nest are turned into ashes, from which a new phoenix arises.

Draw a vertical line to mark the center of the phoenix.

Sketch a small circle for the head.

Draw a large oval for the body.

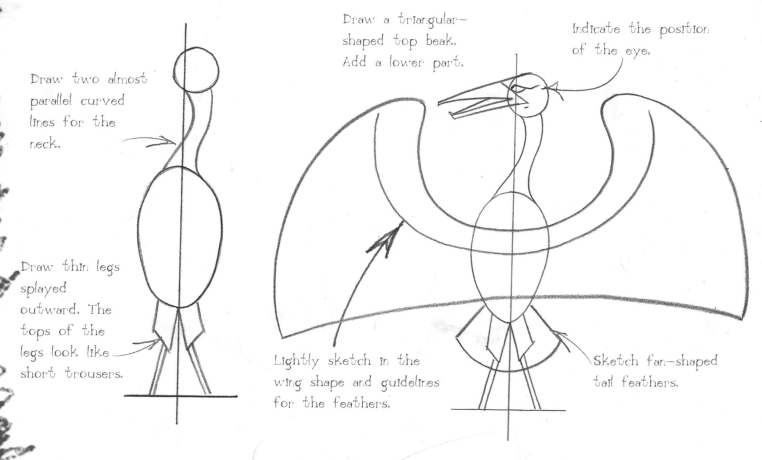

Draw two almost parallel curved lines for the neck.

Draw thin legs splayed outward. The tops of the legs look like short trousers.

Draw a triangular-shaped top beak. Add a lower part.

Indicate the position of the eye.

Lightly sketch in the wing shape and guidelines for the feathers.

Sketch fan-shaped tail feathers.

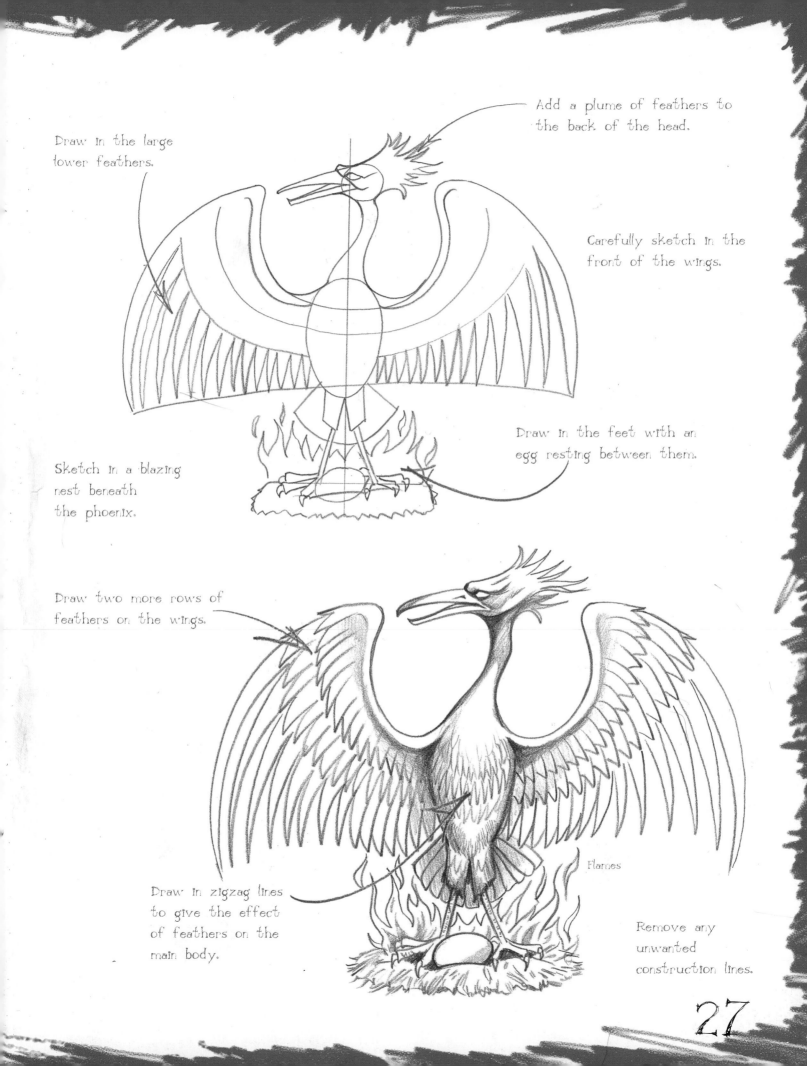

Add a plume of feathers to the back of the head.

Draw in the large lower feathers.

Carefully sketch in the front of the wings.

Draw in the feet with an egg resting between them.

Sketch in a blazing nest beneath the phoenix.

Draw two more rows of feathers on the wings.

Flames

Draw in zigzag lines to give the effect of feathers on the main body.

Remove any unwanted construction lines.

27

Troll

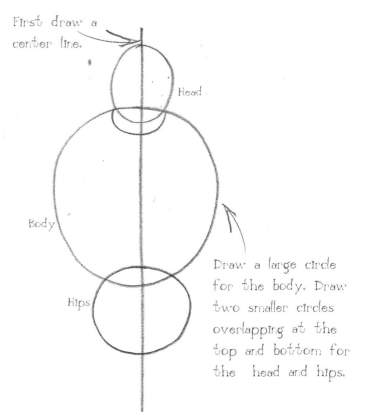

The large mountain troll features in many folk tales. It is said to be a foul—smelling creature that is dim—witted but powerful. Trolls are aggressive toward humans and carry a crude, primitive club as a weapon.

First draw a center line.

Head

Body

Hips

Draw a large circle for the body. Draw two smaller circles overlapping at the top and bottom for the head and hips.

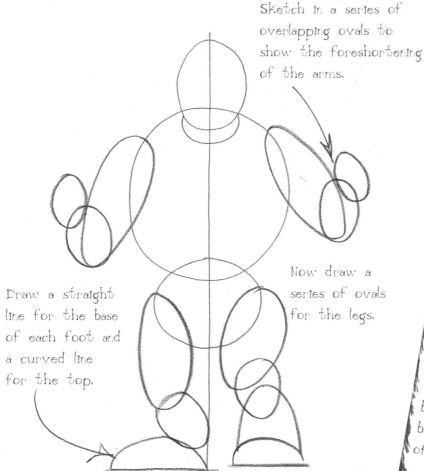

Sketch in a series of overlapping ovals to show the foreshortening of the arms.

Now draw a series of ovals for the legs.

Draw a straight line for the base of each foot and a curved line for the top.

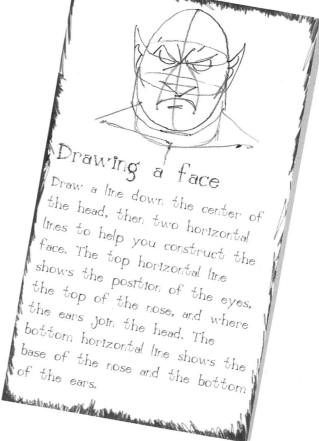

Drawing a face

Draw a line down the center of the head, then two horizontal lines to help you construct the face. The top horizontal line shows the position of the eyes, the top of the nose, and where the ears join the head. The bottom horizontal line shows the base of the nose and the bottom of the ears.

28

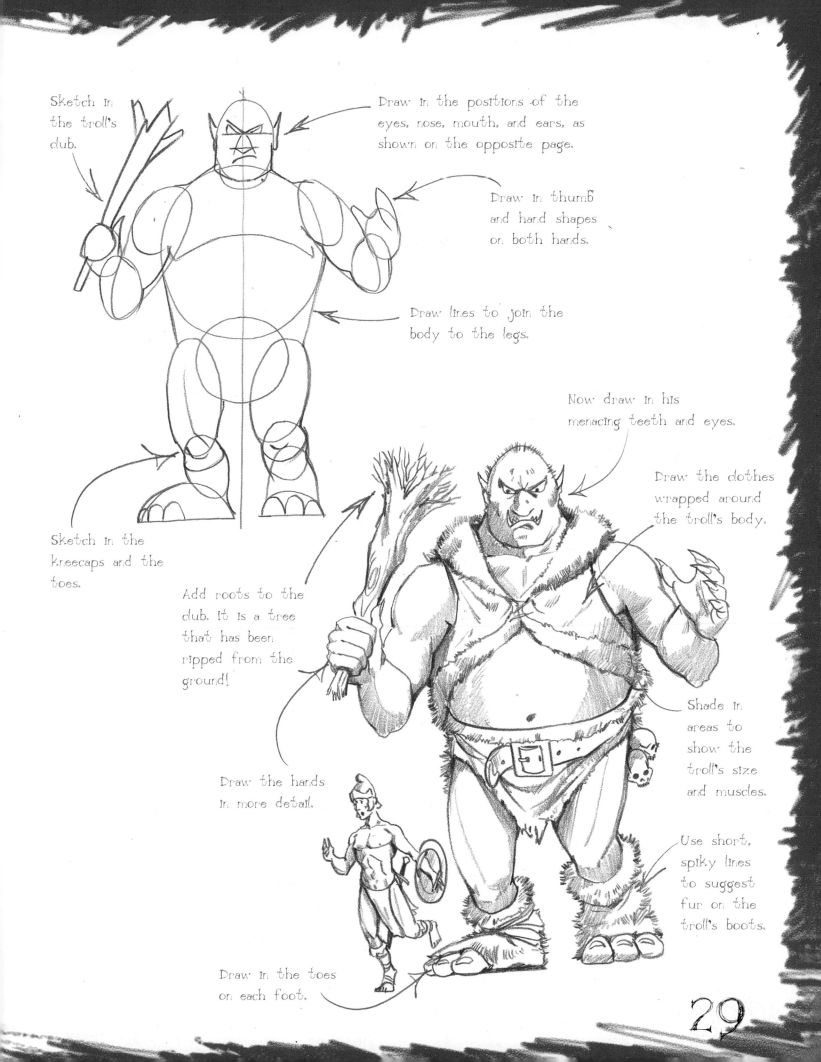

Sketch in the troll's club.

Draw in the positions of the eyes, nose, mouth, and ears, as shown on the opposite page.

Draw in thumb and hand shapes on both hands.

Draw lines to join the body to the legs.

Now draw in his menacing teeth and eyes.

Draw the clothes wrapped around the troll's body.

Sketch in the kneecaps and the toes.

Add roots to the club. It is a tree that has been ripped from the ground!

Draw the hands in more detail.

Shade in areas to show the troll's size and muscles.

Use short, spiky lines to suggest fur on the troll's boots.

Draw in the toes on each foot.

Unicorn

T he unicorn is the fabulous horse with a twisted horn on its head. It is said to be fierce yet good, a selfless, solitary, but always beautiful creature. The ancient Greeks thought that unicorns lived in India.

Above the body, draw a circle for the head and two lines to form the neck.

Head

Back

Rear

Front

Belly

First draw two circles, one slightly larger than the other. Draw in lines for the back and the belly.

Sketch in the muzzle by drawing a smaller circle and then joining it to the head with two lines.

Add ears.

Curved lines around the body and the base of the neck make your drawing look more three—dimensional.

Draw in the legs, using circles to show the positions of the joints.

Curve the belly line upward.

Using a mirror

Hold your picture up to a mirror to look at its reflection. This will help you see any mistakes in your drawing.

The hooves are semicircles.

Make your construction lines curved to show the unicorn's muscle structure.

Sketch in the eyes, nostrils, and horn. Add the unicorn's mane.

Draw more detail on the unicorn's horn.

Sketch in the shape of the tail.

The mane is drawn using random jagged shapes flowing backward.

Add more detail to the head.

Draw in the tail hair with curved lines flowing backward.

Add detail and shading to the hooves. Leave some areas white as highlights.

Shade in areas where light does not reach to give a three-dimensional look.

Glossary

chiaroscuro (kee-AHR-uh-skyur-oh) The use of light and dark to give a dramatic three-dimensional effect.

composition (kom-puh-ZIH-shun) The positioning of a picture on the drawing paper.

construction lines (kun-STRUK-shun LYNZ) Guidelines used in the early stages of a drawing.

fixative (FIK-suh-tiv) A type of resin used to spray over a finished drawing to prevent smudging. Fixatives should be used under adult supervision.

focal point (FOH-kul POYNT) A central point of interest.

foreshortening (for-SHOR-ten-ing) The way an object is seen in perspective when angled toward the viewer. The nearer parts look larger than the farther-away parts.

negative space (NEH-guh-tiv SPAYS) The empty space around a drawn shape.

proportion (pruh-POR-shun) The correct relationship of scale between parts of a drawing.

three-dimensional (three-deh-MENCH-nul) Having an effect of depth, so as to look lifelike or real, rather than flat.

vanishing point (VA-nish-ing POYNT) The place in a perspective drawing where parallel lines seem to meet.

Index

C
centaur 14-15
charcoal 10-11
chiaroscuro 16
composition 9, 15
crayons 10-11
cross-hatching 10, 11

D
dragon 16-17

F
faces 28
fixative 11

G
gryphon 18-19

H
Hydra 20-21

L
light 9, 16, 21, 31

M
materials 10-11
Minotaur 22-23
mirrors 30

N
negative space 18

P
Pegasus 24-25
pencils 11
pens 11
perspective 6-7
phoenix 26-27
proportion 24

S
sketching, sketchbook 12-13

T
three-dimensional drawing 6, 9, 30-31
troll 28-29
two-point perspective 7

U
unicorn 30-31

V
vanishing points 6-7

Web Sites

Due to the changing nature of Internet links, PowerKids Press has developed an online list of Web sites related to the subject of this book. This site is updated regularly. Please use this link to access the list:
www.powerkidslinks.com/htd/magmyth/